LET'S STARTED

THE JOURNEY

INTERNET OF THINGS

*"This **eBook** covers all the essential topics and will help clarify your concepts. It's a valuable resource for preparing for **university / college exams** and Software Development"*

- PRANAY BHUTE

ABOUT THE AUTHORS

Pranay Bhute

My name is Pranay Bhute and I have a passion for education and knowledge sharing. I love reading books and writing to help people access information easily. As an educator, I believe in the power of knowledge to transform lives and empower individuals. I strive to make complex topics simple and interesting so that anyone can benefit from them. My goal is to inspire a love of learning and a thirst for knowledge in others. I enjoy connecting with people and helping them achieve their educational goals.

Meet Pranay Bhute, a passionate educator, avid reader, and dedicated author. With a love for both writing and reading, Pranay has made it his mission to share knowledge and inspire others through his words. As an educator, he thrives on helping others learn and grow, making complex topics easy to understand.

"Stay connected! Follow me on

insta – ibhutepranay

linkedIn- ibhutepranay

Acknowledgment Section:

"This book is prepared using guidance and informational support provided by various sources, including OpenAI's assistant."

UNIT -1

Introduction to IoT

Definition of IoT

The **Internet of Things (IoT)** refers to a network of interconnected physical devices, sensors, software, and other technologies that communicate and exchange data over the internet without requiring human intervention. These devices can range from simple household appliances to complex industrial tools.

Key Points:

- IoT enables seamless communication between devices.
- It plays a vital role in automating processes and improving efficiency in various fields like healthcare, agriculture, transportation, and more.

Characteristics of IoT

IoT has several defining characteristics that make it unique and widely applicable:

1. **Interconnectivity**:
Devices in IoT can connect and communicate with each other

via the internet. This allows data sharing between a vast number of devices globally.

2. **Automation**:

   IoT systems reduce the need for human intervention by automating processes. For example, smart home systems can adjust lighting or temperature automatically based on environmental conditions.

3. **Scalability**:

   IoT frameworks can accommodate an increasing number of devices without compromising performance. This is essential for industries where thousands of sensors are deployed.

4. **Data Analytics**:

   IoT devices collect large volumes of data, which can be analyzed to derive insights, improve processes, or make predictions.

5. **Dynamic Nature**:

   IoT systems continuously update and adapt based on real-time data from connected devices.

6. **Heterogeneity**:

   IoT supports different types of devices and networks, which may use various protocols but still function cohesively.

7. **Security and Privacy**:

   As IoT devices handle sensitive data, ensuring security and

privacy is crucial. This includes data encryption and secure authentication mechanisms.

IoT Conceptual Framework

The **IoT Conceptual Framework** outlines how various components interact within an IoT system. It serves as a blueprint for understanding the structure and functioning of IoT ecosystems.

Key Components of IoT Framework:

1. **Perception Layer (Sensing Layer)**:
    - This layer consists of sensors and actuators.
    - **Purpose**: To collect data from the environment or devices.
    - **Example**: Temperature sensors, motion detectors.
2. **Network Layer**:
    - Responsible for transmitting data collected by sensors to other layers.
    - Uses technologies like Wi-Fi, Bluetooth, ZigBee, or cellular networks.

3. **Data Processing Layer**:
    - Processes the data received from the network layer.
    - Includes cloud computing, edge computing, and data analytics platforms.

4. **Application Layer**:
    - Delivers specific services and functionalities to end-users based on processed data.
    - Examples include smart home apps, industrial automation dashboards, etc.

5. **Security Layer**:
    - Protects data integrity, ensures secure communication, and maintains user privacy.
    - Uses encryption, authentication, and secure protocols.

Advantages of IoT

1. **Automation and Control**:
    - Reduces human effort by automating repetitive tasks.
    - Example: Automatic switching off lights in a smart home.

2. **Improved Efficiency**:
    - Real-time data analysis helps in optimizing processes.
    - Example: Monitoring machine performance in factories.
3. **Cost Savings**:
    - Early detection of faults through IoT devices minimizes repair costs.
    - Example: Predictive maintenance in industries.
4. **Enhanced User Experience**:
    - IoT provides personalized services, improving the overall user experience.
    - Example: Smart fitness devices that track health metrics.
5. **Better Decision Making**:
    - Data from IoT devices provide actionable insights for decision-making.
    - **Example**: Traffic management systems based on real-time traffic data.

Disadvantages of IoT

1. **Security Risks**:

- IoT devices are prone to hacking if not properly secured.
- Example: Unauthorized access to smart home systems.

2. **Privacy Concerns**:
   - As IoT collects a vast amount of data, privacy can be compromised.
   - Example: Tracking user behavior without consent.

3. **High Implementation Cost**:
   - Setting up IoT infrastructure involves significant initial investment.
   - Example: Installing IoT-enabled industrial systems.

4. **Complexity**:
   - Managing and maintaining large IoT ecosystems can be challenging.

5. **Dependency on the Internet**:
   - IoT systems rely heavily on internet connectivity. Any disruption can halt their functionality.

Hindi Explanation

IoT की परिभाषा

इंटरनेट ऑफ थिंग्स (IoT) एक ऐसा नेटवर्क है जिसमें भौतिक डिवाइस, सेंसर, सॉफ़्टवेयर और अन्य तकनीकें आपस में इंटरनेट के माध्यम से बिना मानव हस्तक्षेप के डेटा का आदान-प्रदान करती हैं। ये डिवाइस साधारण घरेलू उपकरणों से लेकर जटिल औद्योगिक उपकरणों तक हो सकते हैं।

IoT की विशेषताएं

1. **इंटरकनेक्टिविटी**:
   IoT डिवाइस एक-दूसरे से कनेक्ट होकर डेटा साझा कर सकते हैं।
2. **स्वचालन (Automation)**:
   IoT प्रक्रियाओं को स्वचालित करता है। जैसे, स्मार्ट होम सिस्टम अपने आप तापमान नियंत्रित कर सकते हैं।
3. **स्केलेबिलिटी**:
   IoT में बड़ी संख्या में डिवाइस जोड़ने की क्षमता होती है।
4. **डेटा एनालिटिक्स**:
   IoT डिवाइस से एकत्र डेटा का विश्लेषण करके महत्वपूर्ण जानकारी प्राप्त की जा सकती है।

डायनेमिक नेचर:
IoT सिस्टम लगातार वास्तविक समय के डेटा के आधार पर अपडेट होते रहते हैं।

IoT की परिकल्पना

IoT के ढांचे में पाँच मुख्य परतें होती हैं:

1. **परसेप्शन लेयर**: डेटा एकत्र करने के लिए।
2. **नेटवर्क लेयर**: डेटा को एक स्थान से दूसरे स्थान तक भेजने के लिए।
3. **प्रोसेसिंग लेयर**: डेटा का विश्लेषण और प्रोसेसिंग।
4. **एप्लिकेशन लेयर**: उपयोगकर्ता सेवाएं प्रदान करना।
5. **सुरक्षा परत**: डेटा सुरक्षा सुनिश्चित करना।

फायदे

1. **स्वचालन और नियंत्रण**
2. **बेहतर दक्षता**
3. **लागत में कमी**
4. **उन्नत उपयोगकर्ता अनुभव**
5. **बेहतर निर्णय लेना**

नुकसान

1. **सुरक्षा जोखिम**
2. **गोपनीयता की चिंता**
3. **उच्च लागत**
4. **जटिलता**
5. **इंटरनेट पर निर्भरता**

IoT Architectural View

Definition:

IoT architecture refers to the structure that defines how various components of an IoT system interact and function together to deliver seamless connectivity and automation.

Key Layers of IoT Architecture:

1. **Perception Layer:**
    - Collects data from the environment through sensors.
    - Example: Temperature sensors in a smart home.

2. **Network Layer:**
    - Transfers collected data to storage or cloud platforms.
    - Example: Data transmission via Wi-Fi or cellular networks.

3. **Processing Layer:**
    - Processes the data using algorithms for decision-making.
    - Example: Analyzing temperature data to adjust the thermostat.

4. **Application Layer:**

- Provides an interface for users to interact with the IoT system.
- Example: Mobile apps for controlling smart home devices.

Advantages of IoT Architecture:

- Ensures efficient communication between devices.
- Simplifies the implementation of complex IoT systems.

Disadvantages:

- High setup cost for multi-layered architecture.
- Requires skilled professionals for maintenance.

Physical Design of IoT

Definition:

Physical design of IoT refers to the tangible components or hardware involved in IoT systems, such as sensors, actuators, and devices.

Key Components:

1. **Sensors:**
   - Collect real-time data from the environment.
   - Example: Temperature, humidity, and motion sensors.

2. **Actuators:**
   - Perform actions based on processed data.
   - Example: A smart light turning on automatically.

3. **IoT Devices:**
   - Embedded systems that combine sensors and actuators.
   - Example: Smart thermostats, smartwatches.

Advantages:

- Provides the necessary interface for data collection and action.
- Helps in real-time monitoring and control.

Disadvantages:

- Physical devices are prone to wear and tear.
- Replacement or upgrades can be costly.

Logical Design of IoT

Definition:

Logical design focuses on the abstract or functional view of an IoT system, including the protocols, interfaces, and methods of data processing.

Key Elements:

1. **Data Processing Units:**

    - Handle data collection, storage, and analysis.

    - Example: Cloud computing platforms like AWS.

2. **Communication Protocols:**

    - Define how data is transmitted between devices.

    - Example: MQTT, HTTP, and CoAP.

3. **Software Interfaces:**

    - Facilitate interaction between users and IoT systems.

    - Example: User-friendly mobile applications.

Advantages:

- Enables efficient data flow and decision-making.
- Provides flexibility in system upgrades.

Disadvantages:

- Vulnerable to cyber-attacks due to reliance on software.
- Requires robust cybersecurity measures.

Applications of IoT

Definition:

IoT applications refer to the practical use cases where IoT technology improves efficiency and provides innovative solutions.

Key Application Areas:

1. **Smart Homes:**
    - Automates home appliances like lights, fans, and security systems.
    - Example: Alexa and Google Home.

2. **Healthcare:**
   - Monitors patient health remotely using wearable devices.
   - Example: Fitness trackers like Fitbit.

3. **Agriculture:**
   - IoT devices monitor soil moisture and weather conditions to optimize farming.
   - Example: Automated irrigation systems.

4. **Industrial IoT (IIoT):**
   - Enhances industrial operations through predictive maintenance and automation.
   - Example: Smart factories.

Advantages:

- Improves efficiency and productivity across sectors.
- Enhances the quality of life with smart systems.

Disadvantages:

- Dependency on technology can lead to failures in critical systems.

- Data privacy and security remain major concerns.

IoT Architectural View (IoT का आर्किटेक्चरल व्यू)

Definition (परिभाषा):

IoT आर्किटेक्चर का मतलब है वो सिस्टम जो ये बताता है कि IoT के सारे डिवाइस और कंपोनेंट्स आपस में कैसे काम करते हैं।

Main Layers (मुख्य परतें):

1. **Perception Layer (परसेप्शन लेयर):**

    - Sensors और actuators इसी परत में आते हैं।
    - Example: Temperature sensor जो तापमान नापता है।

2. **Network Layer (नेटवर्क लेयर):**

    - Data को sensors से server या cloud तक पहुंचाती है।
    - Example: Wi-Fi या Bluetooth के जरिए डेटा भेजना।

3. **Processing Layer (प्रोसेसिंग लेयर):**

    - Data को analyze करके decisions लेती है।

- Example: Smart AC जो temperature के हिसाब से काम करता है।

4. **Application Layer (एप्लिकेशन लेयर):**
    - User को एक interface देती है जिससे वो devices को control कर सकते हैं।
    - Example: Mobile apps जैसे Alexa।

Advantages (फायदे):

- Devices के बीच smooth communication।
- Complex IoT systems को आसानी से manage कर सकते हैं।

Disadvantages (नुकसान):

- Setup महंगा होता है।
- Maintenance के लिए skilled लोग चाहिए।

---

2. Physical Design of IoT (IoT का फिजिकल डिज़ाइन)

Definition (परिभाषा):

Physical design में IoT के hardware components आते हैं जैसे sensors, actuators, और devices। ये वो चीज़ें हैं जो real-world data को collect और control करती हैं।

Main Components (मुख्य घटक):

1. **Sensors (सेंसर):**

    - Environment से data collect करते हैं।
    - Example: Light sensor जो रोशनी detect करता है।

2. **Actuators (एक्चुएटर्स):**

    - Collected data के हिसाब से action perform करते हैं।
    - Example: Fan जो temperature बढ़ने पर automatically चालू हो जाता है।

3. **IoT Devices (IoT डिवाइस):**

    - Sensors और actuators को combine करते हैं।
    - Example: Smartwatch जो आपकी heartbeat monitor करता है।

Advantages (फायदे):

- Real-time data collection और monitoring।
- Daily tasks automated हो जाते हैं।

Disadvantages (नुकसान):

- Devices खराब हो सकते हैं।
- Maintenance और replacement costly हो सकते हैं।

---

3. Logical Design of IoT (IoT का लॉजिकल डिज़ाइन)

Definition (परिभाषा):

Logical design में IoT system के functional components आते हैं, जैसे data processing units, protocols, और interfaces।

Main Elements (मुख्य घटक):

1. **Data Processing Units (डाटा प्रोसेसिंग यूनिट्स):**
    - Collected data को analyze और store करती हैं।
    - Example: Cloud platforms जैसे AWS।

2. **Communication Protocols (कम्युनिकेशन प्रोटोकॉल्स):**
    - Devices के बीच data transfer के rules define करते हैं।
    - Example: MQTT, HTTP।

3. **Software Interfaces (सॉफ्टवेयर इंटरफेसेस):**
    - User को IoT system से interact करने का तरीका देती हैं।

- Example: Mobile app।

Advantages (फायदे):

- Data का efficient flow और processing।
- Flexible system upgrades।

Disadvantages (नुकसान):

- Cyber attacks का खतरा।
- High security की जरूरत होती है।

---

4. Applications of IoT (IoT के उपयोग)

Definition (परिभाषा):

IoT applications real-world में IoT technology का practical use हैं। ये हमारे काम को आसान और efficient बनाते हैं।

Main Applications (मुख्य उपयोग):

1. **Smart Homes (स्मार्ट होम्स):**
   - घर के devices जैसे lights और AC को automate करता है।
   - Example: Google Home।

2. **Healthcare (हेल्थकेयर):**

- मरीज की health को remotely monitor करता है।
- Example: Fitbit जो आपकी daily activity track करता है।

3. **Agriculture (खेती):**
    - Soil और weather को monitor करके farming को efficient बनाता है।
    - Example: Automatic irrigation system।

4. **Industrial IoT (IIoT):**
    - Factories में machines को automate और monitor करता है।
    - Example: Smart factories।

Advantages (फायदे):

- Productivity और efficiency बढ़ती है।
- Human effort कम होता है।

Disadvantages (नुकसान):

- High dependency on technology।
- Data privacy का issue हो सकता है।

Machine-to-Machine (M2M) Communication

Definition:

M2M refers to direct communication between devices without human intervention. It enables devices to exchange data and make decisions autonomously.

Key Features:

- **Automated Communication:** Devices can share data and instructions automatically.

- **Real-time Data Transmission:** Provides instant communication, crucial for time-sensitive applications.

- **Scalability:** Can connect a large number of devices efficiently.

Applications:

- **Healthcare:** Remote monitoring of patients using wearable devices.

- **Smart Homes:** Devices like smart thermostats and lights communicate to optimize energy usage.

- **Industrial Automation:** Machines exchange data to streamline production processes.

Advantages:

- Reduces human intervention and improves efficiency.
- Enables faster decision-making.

Disadvantages:

- High setup and maintenance costs.
- Potential security risks due to increased device connectivity.

Software Defined Networking (SDN) and Network Function Virtualization (NFV) for IoT

SDN (Software Defined Networking):

SDN centralizes network control by separating the control plane from the data plane, making it easier to manage large IoT networks.

NFV (Network Function Virtualization):

NFV virtualizes network functions such as firewalls and load balancers, allowing them to run on software instead of specialized hardware.

Key Features of SDN and NFV:

- **SDN:** Provides dynamic and centralized control of the network.

- **NFV:** Reduces hardware costs and increases deployment flexibility.

Applications in IoT:

- **Dynamic Resource Allocation:** Used in smart grids and traffic management.
- **Network Optimization:** Improves data flow in large IoT systems.

Advantages:

- **SDN:** Simplifies network management and enhances scalability.
- **NFV:** Reduces capital and operational expenses.

Disadvantages:

- Complex initial setup.
- Security vulnerabilities due to centralized control.

Data Storage in IoT

Definition:

In IoT systems, vast amounts of data generated by devices must be stored efficiently for processing and analysis.

Types of IoT Data Storage:

1. **Cloud Storage:**
    - Stores data on centralized servers.
    - Accessible from anywhere with an internet connection.
    - Examples: AWS, Google Cloud.

2. **Edge Storage:**
    - Data is stored locally on the IoT device or a nearby server.
    - Reduces latency and improves real-time data processing.

Key Features:

- **Scalability:** Easily accommodates large volumes of data.
- **Reliability:** Ensures data is available even in case of device failure.

Advantages:

- Offers remote access to data.
- Provides secure and cost-effective storage solutions.

Disadvantages:

- Requires continuous internet connectivity for cloud storage.
- High potential for data breaches.

IoT Cloud-Based Services

Definition:

IoT cloud-based services provide platforms for data storage, real-time data processing, and application deployment.

Types of Cloud-Based Services:

1. **Infrastructure as a Service (IaaS):**
   - Offers virtualized computing resources.
   - Example: Amazon EC2.

2. **Platform as a Service (PaaS):**

- Provides a platform for developing, testing, and deploying applications.
- Example: Microsoft Azure.

3. **Software as a Service (SaaS):**
    - Offers ready-to-use software over the internet.
    - Example: Google Workspace.

Applications:

- **Smart Cities:** Used for managing traffic and energy efficiently.
- **Healthcare:** Enables remote patient monitoring and data analysis.

Advantages:

- **Scalability:** Easily handles growing data and user demands.
- **Cost Efficiency:** Reduces infrastructure costs.

Disadvantages:

- Dependency on internet connectivity.
- Privacy and security concerns related to data storage.

UNIT-3

Design Principles for Web Connectivity

Web Communication Protocols for Connected Devices:

- Web communication protocols are the fundamental rules that enable communication between devices over the internet. These protocols govern how devices send and receive data across networks. The protocols ensure that devices can connect and exchange information securely, efficiently, and reliably.

- **HTTP (Hypertext Transfer Protocol)**: The most commonly used protocol for data communication over the web.

- **HTTPS (Hypertext Transfer Protocol Secure)**: An encrypted version of HTTP, ensuring secure communication.

- **WebSockets**: A protocol that enables two-way communication between a server and a client over a single, long-lived connection.

Message Communication Protocols for Connected Devices:

- These protocols define how messages are exchanged between devices. They ensure that devices understand each other's messages and perform the correct actions.

- **SOAP (Simple Object Access Protocol)**: A protocol for exchanging structured information in the implementation of web services. SOAP messages are typically exchanged over HTTP or SMTP. It uses XML for message formatting.

- **REST (Representational State Transfer)**: A lightweight alternative to SOAP, REST is an architectural style for building web services. It uses standard HTTP methods like GET, POST, PUT, and DELETE. RESTful APIs are widely used because they are simple and scalable.

SOAP (Simple Object Access Protocol):

- SOAP is a protocol used for exchanging structured information in the form of XML documents. It is platform-independent and allows for communication between devices or services over the internet. SOAP requires more overhead compared to REST and typically uses HTTP or SMTP for message transmission.

- **Advantages of SOAP**:

- Platform and language independent.
- Provides built-in error handling and security.
- Supports complex operations and transactions.

- **Disadvantages of SOAP**:
    - More overhead in terms of message format and processing.
    - Less flexible compared to REST.

REST (Representational State Transfer):

- REST is an architectural style, not a protocol, that relies on standard HTTP methods. It uses a stateless architecture, meaning that each request from a client to a server must contain all the necessary information for the server to understand and process the request.

- **Advantages of REST**:
    - Lightweight and easier to implement than SOAP.
    - More scalable and flexible.
    - Uses standard HTTP methods.

- **Disadvantages of REST**:
    - Less robust error handling.
    - Security features depend on the implementation.

HTTP Restful and Web Sockets:

- **HTTP RESTful**: RESTful services are based on the HTTP protocol. They are stateless, meaning each request contains all the information needed to perform an action. RESTful APIs are fast, simple, and rely on HTTP for communication, making them ideal for mobile apps, web applications, and other lightweight communication.

- **Web Sockets**: WebSockets enable two-way communication over a single, long-lasting connection between the client and server. Unlike HTTP, which is request-response based, WebSockets allow real-time data exchange, making it ideal for applications that require constant data updates (e.g., live chats, gaming, and stock market updates).

Hindi Explanation (Simple)

- **1. Web Communication Protocols for Connected Devices:**

- वेब कम्युनिकेशन प्रोटोकॉल्स वे नियम होते हैं, जो डिवाइसों के बीच इंटरनेट के जरिए डेटा संचारित करने के लिए होते हैं। ये प्रोटोकॉल्स यह सुनिश्चित करते हैं कि डिवाइस एक-दूसरे से सुरक्षित, कुशल और विश्वसनीय तरीके से कनेक्ट और डेटा एक्सचेंज कर सकें।

- **HTTP (Hypertext Transfer Protocol)**: सबसे सामान्य प्रोटोकॉल है, जिसका उपयोग वेब पर डेटा संचार के लिए किया जाता है।

- **HTTPS (Hypertext Transfer Protocol Secure)**: HTTP का एक सुरक्षित संस्करण, जो एन्क्रिप्टेड कनेक्शन प्रदान करता है।

- **WebSockets**: एक प्रोटोकॉल है, जो एक लंबे समय तक चलने वाले कनेक्शन पर सर्वर और क्लाइंट के बीच दो-तरफा संचार की अनुमति देता है।

- **2. Message Communication Protocols for Connected Devices:**

- यह प्रोटोकॉल्स यह तय करते हैं कि डिवाइसों के बीच संदेश कैसे आदान-प्रदान किए जाएंगे। ये प्रोटोकॉल्स यह सुनिश्चित करते हैं कि डिवाइसों को एक-दूसरे के संदेश समझ में आएं और वे सही तरीके से कार्रवाई करें।

- **SOAP (Simple Object Access Protocol)**: यह एक प्रोटोकॉल है, जिसका उपयोग वेब सेवाओं में संरचित जानकारी को एक स्थान से दूसरे स्थान तक भेजने के लिए किया जाता है। SOAP संदेशों का आदान-प्रदान आमतौर पर HTTP या SMTP के जरिए होता है।

- **REST (Representational State Transfer)**: SOAP के मुकाबले हल्का और सरल, REST एक आर्किटेक्चरल शैली है, जो वेब सेवाओं के निर्माण में उपयोग होती है। इसमें HTTP के GET, POST, PUT और DELETE जैसे सामान्य मेथड्स का उपयोग किया जाता है। RESTful APIs का उपयोग अधिक किया जाता है क्योंकि ये सरल और स्केलेबल होती हैं।

- **3. SOAP (Simple Object Access Protocol):**

- SOAP एक प्रोटोकॉल है, जो XML डॉक्युमेंट्स के रूप में संरचित जानकारी का आदान-प्रदान करता है। यह प्लेटफ़ॉर्म-स्वतंत्र होता है और डिवाइसों या सेवाओं के बीच इंटरनेट पर संचार की अनुमति देता है। SOAP में REST के मुकाबले अधिक ओवरहेड होता है और यह आमतौर पर HTTP या SMTP का उपयोग करता है।

- **SOAP के फायदे**:

    - प्लेटफ़ॉर्म और भाषा स्वतंत्र।
    - इसमें इन-बिल्ट एरर हैंडलिंग और सुरक्षा होती है।
    - जटिल ऑपरेशन्स और ट्रांजेक्शन्स को सपोर्ट करता है।

- **SOAP के नुकसान**:

    - संदेश के स्वरूप और प्रसंस्करण के संदर्भ में अधिक ओवरहेड होता है।
    - REST के मुकाबले कम लचीलापन होता है।

- **4. REST (Representational State Transfer):**
- REST एक आर्किटेक्चरल स्टाइल है, जो सामान्य HTTP मेथड्स पर निर्भर करता है। यह स्टेटलेस आर्किटेक्चर का पालन करता है, अर्थात हर क्लाइंट से सर्वर तक भेजी गई रिक्वेस्ट में सारी जानकारी होती है, जिससे सर्वर उसे समझ सके और उसे प्रोसेस कर सके।

- **REST के फायदे**:
    - SOAP की तुलना में हल्का और सरल।
    - अधिक स्केलेबल और लचीला।
    - सामान्य HTTP मेथड्स का उपयोग करता है।

- **REST के नुकसान**:
    - कम मजबूत एरर हैंडलिंग।
    - सुरक्षा विशेषताएँ कार्यान्वयन पर निर्भर होती हैं।

- **5. HTTP Restful और WebSockets:**

- **HTTP RESTful**: RESTful सेवाएँ HTTP प्रोटोकॉल पर आधारित होती हैं। ये स्टेटलेस होती हैं, यानी हर रिक्वेस्ट में उस क्रिया को पूरा करने के लिए सारी जानकारी होती है। RESTful APIs तेज़, सरल और HTTP पर संचार करती हैं, जो इन्हें मोबाइल ऐप्स, वेब एप्लिकेशंस और अन्य हल्के संचार के लिए आदर्श बनाता है।

- **WebSockets**: WebSockets दो-तरफा संचार की अनुमति देते हैं, जो क्लाइंट और सर्वर के बीच एक लंबे समय तक चलने वाले कनेक्शन पर होता है। HTTP के मुकाबले WebSockets रीयल-टाइम डेटा एक्सचेंज की अनुमति देते हैं, जो लाइव चैट, गेमिंग और स्टॉक मार्केट अपडेट्स जैसे अनुप्रयोगों के लिए आदर्श होते हैं।

Internet Connectivity Principles

Internet Connectivity:

- Internet connectivity refers to the capability of a device or system to connect to the internet and communicate with other devices or systems. It forms the backbone for data transfer and exchange over the internet, enabling various applications such as browsing, communication, and IoT devices functioning.

- **Types of Internet Connectivity**:

- **Wired Connectivity**: Uses physical cables like fiber optics, Ethernet, etc.
- **Wireless Connectivity**: Uses radio waves or other wireless technologies like Wi-Fi, Bluetooth, 4G/5G, etc.
- **Satellite Connectivity**: Used for remote or hard-to-reach areas, using satellites for data transmission.

- **Features of Internet Connectivity**:
  - **High-speed access**: Enables faster data transmission.
  - **Always-on connection**: Ensures continuous communication.
  - **Reliable service**: Ensures minimal interruptions or downtime.
  - **Scalable**: Can support a growing number of devices and users.

- **Advantages**:
  - **Fast Communication**: Internet connectivity enables real-time communication, making it faster to transfer and receive information.

- - **Global Reach**: It connects devices worldwide, making remote communication and data sharing easier.

  - **Efficient Operation**: Helps businesses and users to efficiently perform tasks remotely.

- **Disadvantages**:

  - **Dependency on Infrastructure**: Requires the right infrastructure, such as networks and equipment, which can be costly.

  - **Security Risks**: Being online poses security threats like hacking, data breaches, etc.

  - **Connectivity Issues**: Internet connections can be unreliable in some areas, leading to interruptions in service.

Internet-Based Communication:

- Internet-based communication involves the transmission of data or information using the internet infrastructure. It can include various communication technologies like email, messaging apps, voice calls, video calls, and IoT communication protocols.

- **Types of Internet-Based Communication**:
    - **Email**: Sending and receiving messages over the internet.
    - **Instant Messaging**: Real-time text communication over the internet.
    - **Voice-over-IP (VoIP)**: Communication via voice over the internet (e.g., Skype, WhatsApp).
    - **Video Conferencing**: Real-time video communication over the internet (e.g., Zoom, Microsoft Teams).
- **Features of Internet-Based Communication**:
    - **Real-time communication**: Instant data exchange.
    - **Global reach**: Connects users across the world.
    - **Cost-effective**: Reduces the cost of communication compared to traditional methods.
- **Advantages**:
    - **Instant Communication**: Allows immediate communication without delays.
    - **Cost-Efficient**: Cuts down on phone bills and traditional communication costs.

- o **Multi-Channel Communication**: Supports text, audio, and video, providing more versatile options.

- **Disadvantages**:

  - o **Privacy Concerns**: Information shared may be at risk due to data breaches or lack of encryption.

  - o **Overload of Communication**: Excessive messages and notifications can lead to information overload.

  - o **Internet Access Dependency**: Without internet access, communication may be disrupted.

IP Addressing in IoT:

- In IoT (Internet of Things), IP addressing is used to identify devices on the network, allowing them to send and receive data over the internet. Each IoT device needs a unique IP address to communicate effectively in the network.

- **Types of IP Addressing**:

  - o **IPv4 (Internet Protocol Version 4)**: The most widely used IP addressing system. It uses a 32-bit address, allowing for approximately 4.3 billion unique addresses.

- **IPv6 (Internet Protocol Version 6)**: A newer system using a 128-bit address, allowing for a vastly larger number of unique IP addresses (over 340 undecillion addresses).

- **Features of IP Addressing in IoT**:
  - **Unique identification**: Every device is uniquely identified within the network.
  - **Routing and Communication**: Ensures that data can be correctly routed to the destination device.
  - **Scalability**: IPv6 provides the scalability needed to accommodate billions of devices in the IoT ecosystem.

- **Advantages**:
  - **Global Identification**: Ensures that every device can be identified globally on the network.
  - **Efficiency in Communication**: Devices can efficiently communicate, avoiding confusion.
  - **Long-term scalability**: IPv6 ensures enough unique addresses for the growing number of IoT devices.

- **Disadvantages**:

- **Complexity**: IPv6 can be difficult to implement for some networks.

- **IPv4 Compatibility**: Transitioning from IPv4 to IPv6 can be time-consuming and challenging.

- **Address Exhaustion**: Though IPv6 solves the address exhaustion issue, many systems still rely on IPv4.

Media Access Control (MAC):

- Media Access Control (MAC) is a protocol that defines how devices on a network access and transmit data over the shared communication medium. In IoT, MAC protocols help manage the flow of data between devices and ensure that communication is efficient and secure.

- **Types of MAC Protocols**:

  - **ALOHA**: A simple and early MAC protocol that allows devices to send data whenever they want. It's inefficient as it doesn't check if the channel is free.

  - **CSMA (Carrier Sense Multiple Access)**: A protocol where devices listen to the channel before sending data to avoid collisions.

- - **TDMA (Time Division Multiple Access)**: Divides time into slots and assigns each device a specific time slot to transmit data, reducing collisions.
  - **FDMA (Frequency Division Multiple Access)**: Divides the frequency spectrum into bands, assigning each device a separate frequency band.
- **Features of Media Access Control**:
  - **Collision avoidance**: Ensures that devices don't send data at the same time, which could cause data loss.
  - **Efficient data transmission**: Helps manage the data flow in a network.
  - **Low latency**: Reduces the delay in sending and receiving data.
- **Advantages**:
  - **Efficient Communication**: Ensures that devices on the network can communicate without data loss.
  - **Reduced Data Collisions**: Protocols like CSMA and TDMA help avoid data collisions, improving efficiency.

- o **Better Resource Management**: Manages bandwidth and other resources effectively.

- **Disadvantages**:

  - o **Channel Congestion**: In some protocols, too many devices trying to communicate at the same time can cause congestion.

  - o **Complexity in Implementation**: Protocols like TDMA and FDMA can be complex to implement and manage.

  - o **Overhead**: Some protocols may require additional overhead to maintain communication.

Hindi Explanation (Simple)

- **1. Internet Connectivity (इंटरनेट कनेक्टिविटी):**

- इंटरनेट कनेक्टिविटी का मतलब है कि कोई डिवाइस या सिस्टम इंटरनेट से जुड़ सकता है और दूसरे डिवाइस या सिस्टम के साथ बात कर सकता है। यह डेटा ट्रांसफर और इंटरनेट पर जानकारी के आदान-प्रदान की प्रक्रिया है, जो वेब ब्राउज़िंग, संचार और IoT डिवाइसों के काम करने में मदद करता है।

- इंटरनेट कनेक्टिविटी के प्रकार:

- **वायर कनेक्टिविटी**: इसमें फिजिकल केबल जैसे फाइबर ऑप्टिक्स, ईथरनेट आदि का उपयोग होता है।

- **वायरलेस कनेक्टिविटी**: इसमें रेडियो वेव्स या अन्य वायरलेस तकनीक जैसे Wi-Fi, Bluetooth, 4G/5G आदि का उपयोग होता है।

- **सैटेलाइट कनेक्टिविटी**: यह दूरस्थ स्थानों पर उपयोग की जाती है, जहाँ अन्य कनेक्टिविटी उपलब्ध नहीं होती है।

- **इंटरनेट कनेक्टिविटी की विशेषताएँ**:

    - **हाई स्पीड एक्सेस**: तेज़ डेटा ट्रांसमिशन के लिए मदद करता है।

    - **हमेशा ऑन कनेक्शन**: यह निरंतर संचार की अनुमति देता है।

    - **विश्वसनीय सेवा**: इसमें कम से कम रुकावट या डाउनटाइम होता है।

    - **स्केलेबल**: यह अधिक उपकरणों और उपयोगकर्ताओं को सपोर्ट करता है।

- **फायदे**:

    - **तेज़ संचार**: इंटरनेट कनेक्टिविटी रियल-टाइम में संचार की अनुमति देती है, जिससे जानकारी जल्दी से ट्रांसफर और प्राप्त होती है।

    - **वैश्विक पहुंच**: यह उपकरणों को दुनिया भर में जोड़ती है, जिससे दूरस्थ संचार और डेटा शेयरिंग आसान हो जाती है।

- ○ **कुशल संचालन**: यह व्यवसायों और उपयोगकर्ताओं को दूरस्थ रूप से काम करने में मदद करता है।

- **नुकसान**:

  - ○ **इन्फ्रास्ट्रक्चर पर निर्भरता**: इसके लिए सही इन्फ्रास्ट्रक्चर, जैसे नेटवर्क और उपकरण, की आवश्यकता होती है, जो महंगा हो सकता है।

  - ○ **सुरक्षा जोखिम**: ऑनलाइन रहने पर सुरक्षा खतरे हो सकते हैं, जैसे हैकिंग, डेटा लीक आदि।

  - ○ **कनेक्टिविटी समस्याएँ**: कुछ क्षेत्रों में इंटरनेट कनेक्शन अविश्वसनीय हो सकते हैं, जिससे सेवा में विघटन हो सकता है।

- **2. Internet-Based Communication (इंटरनेट आधारित संचार):**

- इंटरनेट आधारित संचार में डेटा या जानकारी इंटरनेट के जरिए भेजी जाती है। इसमें कई प्रकार की संचार तकनीकों जैसे ईमेल, मैसेजिंग ऐप्स, वॉयस कॉल्स, वीडियो कॉल्स और IoT संचार प्रोटोकॉल्स शामिल हैं।

- **इंटरनेट आधारित संचार के प्रकार**:

  - ○ **ईमेल**: इंटरनेट के माध्यम से संदेश भेजना और प्राप्त करना।

  - ○ **इंस्टेंट मैसेजिंग**: इंटरनेट पर रियल-टाइम में टेक्स्ट संचार।

- ○ **वॉयस-ओवर-आईपी (VoIP)**: इंटरनेट पर आवाज़ के माध्यम से संचार (जैसे Skype, WhatsApp)।
- ○ **वीडियो कॉन्फ्रेंसिंग**: इंटरनेट के माध्यम से रियल-टाइम वीडियो संचार (जैसे Zoom, Microsoft Teams)।

- **इंटरनेट आधारित संचार की विशेषताएँ**:
  - ○ **रियल-टाइम संचार**: तत्काल डेटा का आदान-प्रदान।
  - ○ **वैश्विक पहुंच**: दुनिया भर के उपयोगकर्ताओं को जोड़ता है।
  - ○ **सस्ती संचार**: पारंपरिक विधियों के मुकाबले संचार की लागत को घटाता है।

- **फायदे**:
  - ○ **तत्काल संचार**: बिना किसी देरी के तुरंत संचार की अनुमति देता है।
  - ○ **सस्ती संचार**: फोन बिल और पारंपरिक संचार लागत को कम करता है।
  - ○ **मल्टी-चैनल संचार**: टेक्स्ट, ऑडियो और वीडियो के लिए अधिक विकल्प प्रदान करता है।

- **नुकसान**:
  - ○ **गोपनीयता के मुद्दे**: डेटा लीक या एन्क्रिप्शन की कमी के कारण साझा की गई जानकारी जोखिम में हो सकती है।

- **सूचना की अधिकता**: अत्यधिक संदेश और नोटिफिकेशन्स जानकारी के बोझ का कारण बन सकते हैं।

- **इंटरनेट एक्सेस पर निर्भरता**: बिना इंटरनेट कनेक्शन के संचार बाधित हो सकता है।

UNIT-3

Sensor Technology

- **Definition**:

    Sensor technology involves the use of sensors to detect physical conditions like temperature, pressure, humidity, motion, and more. These sensors convert physical data into digital information that can be used by IoT devices and applications.

- **Types of Sensors**:

    - **Temperature Sensors**: Measure temperature changes in the environment, e.g., thermocouples and thermistors.

    - **Motion Sensors**: Detect physical movement, e.g., Passive Infrared (PIR) sensors.

    - **Pressure Sensors**: Measure pressure changes applied to an object, e.g., piezoelectric sensors.

    - **Humidity Sensors**: Measure the moisture content in the air.

    - **Gas Sensors**: Detect the presence of various gases like carbon dioxide or methane.

    -

- **Features**:
  - **Real-time Monitoring**: Sensors provide continuous, real-time data.
  - **Automation**: Can trigger automated actions based on sensor data (e.g., turning on a light when motion is detected).
  - **Interconnectivity**: Sensors in IoT devices can communicate and share data across networks.
- **Advantages**:
  - **Accuracy**: Sensors provide precise and accurate measurements.
  - **Cost-effective**: Many sensors are inexpensive and can be deployed in large numbers.
  - **Real-time Data**: Continuous data collection allows for monitoring at all times.
- **Disadvantages**:
  - **Data Overload**: Too much data from multiple sensors can be overwhelming and difficult to process.

- **Battery Life**: Sensors running on batteries can have limited operational time, especially in remote locations.
- **Calibration**: Sensors need regular calibration to maintain accuracy.

Participatory Sensing

- **Definition**:

  Participatory sensing refers to the process of collecting data through the active participation of the public using mobile devices, wearable sensors, and other connected gadgets. This data is then analyzed to gain insights for problem-solving or decision-making.

- **Types of Participatory Sensing**:

  - **Mobile Sensing**: Users' smartphones or wearable devices collect and send data to the system.
  - **Environmental Sensing**: Public participants report data related to environmental factors like air quality, weather, or pollution.

- **Health-related Sensing**: Wearable devices collect health data such as steps, heart rate, or blood pressure.

- **Features**:

    - **Crowdsourced Data**: Involves large-scale data collection through public participation.

    - **Real-time Data**: Enables real-time reporting and monitoring of various factors.

    - **Community-driven**: Empowers communities to gather data and solve local issues collectively.

- **Advantages**:

    - **Cost-Effective**: Large-scale data collection without the need for expensive infrastructure.

    - **Real-time Insights**: Real-time data helps address problems instantly.

    - **Wider Coverage**: Crowdsourcing allows for data collection over a vast area, reaching more diverse regions.

- **Disadvantages**:

- **Data Accuracy**: Public participation may lead to inconsistent or inaccurate data collection.
- **Privacy Concerns**: The sharing of sensitive personal data could raise privacy issues.
- **Data Validation**: Ensuring the authenticity of the data gathered from participants can be challenging.

Industrial IoT (IIoT) and Automotive IoT

Industrial IoT (IIoT)

- **Definition**:
  Industrial IoT (IIoT) refers to the use of IoT devices and sensors in industrial settings such as manufacturing plants, warehouses, and power plants. IIoT helps monitor, control, and automate industrial processes, improving efficiency, safety, and reliability.

- **Types of IIoT Applications**:
  - **Predictive Maintenance**: Using sensors to predict when machines need maintenance, reducing downtime and costs.

- **Asset Tracking**: Monitoring the location and status of machinery and equipment in real-time.
- **Supply Chain Optimization**: Real-time data allows companies to better manage inventory, shipping, and logistics.

• **Features**:

- **Remote Monitoring**: IIoT enables remote monitoring of industrial operations.
- **Automation**: Industrial processes can be automated based on real-time sensor data.
- **Data-Driven Decision Making**: Provides accurate, real-time data for improving operational decisions.

• **Advantages**:

- **Operational Efficiency**: IIoT enhances productivity by automating tasks and minimizing human errors.
- **Cost Reduction**: Helps reduce maintenance costs and prevent unplanned downtime.
- **Real-Time Data**: Provides continuous data flow, improving decision-making.

- **Disadvantages**:
    - **Initial Investment**: Setting up IIoT systems requires high initial costs.
    - **Cybersecurity Risks**: Increased connectivity creates vulnerabilities to cyberattacks.
    - **Complexity**: Integrating IIoT solutions with existing infrastructure can be complex.

Automotive IoT

- **Definition**:
  Automotive IoT refers to the integration of IoT technologies in vehicles, improving safety, efficiency, and driving experience. This includes connected vehicles, autonomous driving systems, and telematics.

- **Types of Automotive IoT Applications**:
    - **Vehicle-to-Vehicle (V2V) Communication**: Allows vehicles to communicate with each other to prevent accidents.
    - **Telematics**: Systems that monitor and track vehicle data like speed, location, and engine health.

- **Autonomous Vehicles**: Self-driving cars use IoT sensors and data to navigate without human intervention.

- **Features**:

  - **Connectivity**: Vehicles communicate with each other and with external systems for real-time traffic and safety information.

  - **Telematics**: Data on vehicle health, location, and driver behavior is collected and transmitted for analysis.

  - **Autonomous Driving**: Vehicles use IoT technology to make driving decisions without human input.

- **Advantages**:

  - **Increased Safety**: IoT-enabled vehicles improve safety features like collision detection and automatic braking.

  - **Fuel Efficiency**: IoT systems help optimize fuel consumption and reduce carbon emissions.

  - **Enhanced Experience**: Connected vehicles offer real-time information on traffic, weather, and vehicle health.

- **Disadvantages**:
  - **Security Risks**: IoT-enabled vehicles are susceptible to hacking and data breaches.
  - **High Cost**: Smart features and connected technologies can increase vehicle prices.
  - **Technology Dependency**: Overreliance on IoT for vehicle operation can create challenges if systems fail.

Sensor Technology (IN HINDI)

- **Sensor Technology** woh technology hai jo physical conditions ko measure karne ke liye sensors ka use karti hai. Ye sensors temperature, motion, pressure, humidity, aur other physical properties ko detect karke unhe data mein convert karte hain, jo baad mein IoT applications mein use hota hai.

- **Types of Sensors**:
    - **Temperature Sensors**: Yeh sensors temperature ko measure karte hain, jaise thermocouples aur thermistors.
    - **Motion Sensors**: Inka use movement ya position ko detect karne ke liye hota hai, jaise PIR (Passive Infrared) sensors.
    - **Pressure Sensors**: Yeh kisi object pe apply hone wale pressure ko measure karte hain, jaise piezoelectric sensors.
    - **Humidity Sensors**: Yeh air mein moisture level ko measure karte hain.

- **Features**:

- **Real-Time Monitoring**: Sensors continuous real-time data provide karte hain.
- **Automation**: Sensors automatic actions ko trigger karte hain based on data.
- **Interconnectivity**: IoT devices mein sensors interconnected hote hain jo data ko share karte hain across different devices.

- **Advantages**:
  - **Accuracy**: Sensors accurate measurements provide karte hain.
  - **Cost-Effective**: Bahut se sensors low-cost hote hain, jo large-scale IoT applications mein use ho sakte hain.
  - **Continuous Data Collection**: Sensors ki madad se 24/7 data collect kiya ja sakta hai.

- **Disadvantages**:
  - **Data Overload**: Excess data generate ho sakta hai jo process karne mein difficult hota hai.
  - **Battery Issues**: Remote areas mein sensor ka battery life limited ho sakta hai.

- **Calibration Needs**: Sensors ko accurate measurements ke liye regularly calibrate karna padta hai.

Participatory Sensing

- **Participatory Sensing** ek aisi technology hai jisme general public apne mobile phones aur devices ke zariye environmental data collect karte hain. Isme users actively participate karte hain aur unka data analyze karke important insights nikale jaate hain, jo problems solve karne mein madad karte hain.

- **Features**:
  - **User-Generated Data**: Public apna data submit karte hain through mobile phones aur other connected devices.
  - **Crowdsourcing**: Data collection ka kaam large number of people mil kar karte hain.
  - **Community Engagement**: Logon ko involve karke issues ko identify kiya jata hai.

- **Advantages**:

- **Cost-Effective**: Large-scale data collection without heavy infrastructure.
- **Real-Time Information**: Public se directly data milne ki wajah se real-time analysis hota hai.
- **Wider Coverage**: Larger area ko cover kiya ja sakta hai kyunki public participation hota hai.

- **Disadvantages**:
  - **Data Accuracy**: Public se data collect karte waqt accuracy issues ho sakte hain.
  - **Privacy Concerns**: Sensitive data ko collect karne se privacy issues ho sakte hain.
  - **Data Validation**: Gathered data ki authenticity verify karna mushkil ho sakta hai.

Industrial IoT (IIoT) and Automotive IoT

- **Industrial IoT (IIoT)** aur **Automotive IoT** applications mein IoT technologies ko industry aur automobiles mein integrate kiya jata hai. Industrial IoT mein machines, sensors, aur devices ko interconnect kiya jata hai taaki operational efficiency aur safety improve ho sake, jabki automotive IoT vehicles mein connectivity, automation, aur safety features ko enhance karta hai.

Industrial IoT (IIoT)

- **Definition**: Industrial IoT ek network hai jisme industrial machines aur devices ko connected kiya jata hai taaki real-time monitoring aur automation ki ja sake.

- **Features**:
    - **Remote Monitoring**: Industrial machines ko remotely monitor kiya ja sakta hai.
    - **Predictive Maintenance**: Sensors ke through machines ki health monitor ki jati hai, jisse unhe repair karne ka time predict ho sakta hai.
    - **Automation**: Industrial processes ko automate kiya ja sakta hai.

- **Advantages**:
    - **Improved Efficiency**: IIoT systems processes ko automate karte hain, jisse operational efficiency badh jati hai.

- **Cost Savings**: Maintenance aur downtime ko reduce karte hain, jo cost savings mein help karta hai.
  - **Better Decision Making**: Real-time data se better decisions liye ja sakte hain.

- **Disadvantages**:
  - **High Initial Costs**: IIoT systems ko install karne ke liye high initial investment hota hai.
  - **Data Security**: Connected devices ke zariye sensitive data leak ho sakta hai.
  - **Complexity**: IIoT systems ko integrate aur manage karna complex ho sakta hai.

Automotive IoT

- **Definition**: Automotive IoT mein vehicles ko smart technologies se integrate kiya jata hai, jo vehicles ko safe, efficient, aur connected banata hai.

- **Features**:
  - **Vehicle-to-Everything (V2X)**: Vehicles dusre vehicles aur infrastructure ke sath communicate karte hain.

- **Telematics**: Vehicle data ko remotely monitor kiya jata hai.
- **Autonomous Vehicles**: Vehicles ko autonomous banane ke liye IoT ka use hota hai.

- **Advantages**:
  - **Safety**: Vehicles mein safety features enhance hote hain, jaise collision detection, automatic braking, etc.
  - **Fuel Efficiency**: IoT-based systems fuel consumption ko optimize karte hain.
  - **Real-Time Tracking**: Vehicles ko real-time track kiya ja sakta hai for better fleet management.

- **Disadvantages**:
  - **Security Risks**: IoT-enabled vehicles mein hacking aur security risks badh jate hain.
  - **High Cost**: Smart features ki wajah se vehicles ka cost kaafi badh jata hai.
  - **Dependence on Technology**: IoT-enabled vehicles highly technology-dependent hote hain, jo failure ka risk create karte hain.

Actuator, Sensor Data Communication Protocols

Definition:

Actuators are devices that perform actions based on the data received from sensors. In IoT systems, they interact with sensors, receive the data, and execute actions such as moving an object or turning on a light. Communication protocols help in the transmission of data between sensors, actuators, and other devices in a network.

- **Types of Actuators**:

    - **Electrical Actuators**: Use electrical energy to perform work, e.g., motors and solenoids.

    - **Pneumatic Actuators**: Use compressed air to move objects, e.g., air cylinders.

    - **Hydraulic Actuators**: Use pressurized fluids to create motion.

- **Communication Protocols**:

    - **MQTT (Message Queuing Telemetry Transport)**: A lightweight protocol used for IoT communication, especially in low-bandwidth scenarios.

- **CoAP (Constrained Application Protocol)**: Designed for simple devices with limited resources, ideal for sensor networks.
- **HTTP (HyperText Transfer Protocol)**: A widely used protocol for communication between clients and servers.

- **Advantages**:
  - **Efficiency**: Allows automated actions based on sensor data.
  - **Real-time Operations**: Facilitates immediate action upon receiving data.
  - **Wide Compatibility**: Can work with different types of sensors and actuators.

- **Disadvantages**:
  - **Power Consumption**: Some actuators consume significant power, especially in large networks.
  - **Latency**: Data communication between sensors, actuators, and networks may have delays.
  - **Complexity**: Managing multiple devices and protocols can become complex.

Radio Frequency Identification (RFID) Technology

Definition:

RFID technology uses electromagnetic fields to automatically identify and track tags attached to objects. These tags contain embedded data that can be read from a distance using an RFID reader. RFID is used for inventory management, asset tracking, and logistics.

- **Types of RFID**:

    - **Passive RFID**: The tag does not have its power source and is activated by the reader's signal.

    - **Active RFID**: The tag has its power source and can transmit signals over longer distances.

    - **Semi-passive RFID**: The tag uses a battery to power the chip, but the reader still powers the communication.

- **Features**:

    - **Contactless Communication**: No physical contact is needed for reading the data.

    - **Fast Data Transmission**: Enables quick transfer of information between the tag and the reader.

- **Long Range**: Active RFID tags can be read from several meters away.

• **Advantages**:

- **Automation**: Automates the identification and tracking of objects.

- **Accuracy**: Reduces human error in inventory and asset management.

- **Durability**: RFID tags are often more durable than barcodes or other tracking methods.

• **Disadvantages**:

- **Cost**: RFID tags, especially active ones, can be expensive.

- **Interference**: Electromagnetic interference can sometimes disrupt RFID communication.

- **Privacy Concerns**: The data on RFID tags could be accessed by unauthorized individuals.

Wireless Sensor Network (WSN) Technology

Definition:

Wireless Sensor Networks (WSNs) consist of a large number of sensor nodes deployed over a wide area to collect data about the environment, such as temperature, humidity, motion, etc. These nodes communicate wirelessly with each other and transmit the data to a central server or a cloud system for analysis.

- **Types of WSN**:
    - **Homogeneous WSN**: All sensor nodes have identical capabilities and operate in the same way.
    - **Heterogeneous WSN**: Sensor nodes have different capabilities and functions.
    - **Mobile WSN**: The sensor nodes are capable of movement and can relocate themselves.
- **Features**:
    - **Energy Efficiency**: WSNs are designed to operate on low power for long durations.
    - **Scalability**: The network can scale up with the addition of more sensor nodes.

- o **Autonomous Operation**: Nodes operate autonomously, transmitting data without human intervention.

- **Advantages**:

  - o **Remote Monitoring**: Can monitor and collect data from hard-to-reach locations.

  - o **Low Cost**: Sensor nodes are typically inexpensive and easy to deploy.

  - o **Real-time Data**: Offers real-time data collection and analysis for immediate action.

- **Disadvantages**:

  - o **Limited Battery Life**: Sensor nodes rely on batteries, and their lifespan is limited.

  - o **Network Reliability**: The network can become unstable if sensor nodes fail or are damaged.

  - o **Data Overload**: Large-scale sensor networks can generate a lot of data that may be difficult to process and analyze.

Hindi Explanation (Hinglish)

Actuator, Sensor Data Communication Protocols

Definition:

Actuator wo devices hote hain jo sensor se data milne par action perform karte hain. IoT mein, actuators sensors se data lete hain aur us par action execute karte hain, jaise kisi light ko on karna ya koi object move karna. Communication protocols wo methods hote hain jo sensor aur actuators ke beech data exchange karte hain.

- **Types of Actuators**:

    - **Electrical Actuators**: Electrical energy se kaam karte hain, jaise motors aur solenoids.

    - **Pneumatic Actuators**: Compressed air ka use karte hain, jaise air cylinders.

    - **Hydraulic Actuators**: Pressurized fluids ka use karte hain motion create karne ke liye.

- **Communication Protocols**:

    - **MQTT (Message Queuing Telemetry Transport)**: Ye ek lightweight protocol hai jo low-bandwidth environments mein kaam karta hai.

- **CoAP (Constrained Application Protocol)**: Ye simple devices ke liye banaya gaya hai, jo limited resources ke sath kaam karte hain.
- **HTTP (HyperText Transfer Protocol)**: Ye widely used protocol hai jo client-server communication ke liye use hota hai.

- **Advantages**:
  - **Efficiency**: Automation ke liye sensor data pe action lene mein madad karta hai.
  - **Real-time Operations**: Data milte hi immediate action perform hota hai.
  - **Wide Compatibility**: Sensors aur actuators ke beech easy integration hoti hai.

- **Disadvantages**:
  - **Power Consumption**: Kuch actuators jyada power consume karte hain, especially large networks mein.
  - **Latency**: Sensors aur actuators ke beech data communication mein thoda time lag sakta hai.

- **Complexity**: Multiple devices aur protocols ko manage karna complex ho sakta hai.

Radio Frequency Identification (RFID) Technology

Definition:
RFID ek technology hai jisme electromagnetic fields ka use karke objects ke tags ko identify aur track kiya jata hai. Ye tags information store karte hain jo RFID reader ke through remotely read ki ja sakti hai. Iska use inventory management, asset tracking aur logistics mein hota hai.

- **Types of RFID**:
    - **Passive RFID**: Tag ka apna power source nahi hota, reader se signal milne par activated hota hai.
    - **Active RFID**: Tag apna power source rakhta hai aur zyada doori tak signal bhej sakta hai.
    - **Semi-passive RFID**: Tag ka battery hota hai jo chip ko power deta hai, lekin communication reader se hota hai.
- **Features**:

- o **Contactless Communication**: Data ko bina kisi physical contact ke read kiya jata hai.

- o **Fast Data Transmission**: Data transfer fast hota hai between tag and reader.

- o **Long Range**: Active RFID tags ko kaafi door se read kiya ja sakta hai.

- **Advantages**:

  - o **Automation**: Object tracking aur identification automated hoti hai.

  - o **Accuracy**: Inventory aur asset management mein human error reduce hota hai.

  - o **Durability**: RFID tags barcodes se zyada durable hote hain.

- **Disadvantages**:

  - o **Cost**: Active RFID tags costly ho sakte hain.

  - o **Interference**: Electromagnetic interference se communication disrupt ho sakti hai.

- **Privacy Concerns**: Unauthorized individuals RFID data access kar sakte hain.

Wireless Sensor Network (WSN) Technology

Definition:

Wireless Sensor Networks (WSN) ek large network hota hai sensor nodes ka, jo widely distributed area mein environmental data collect karte hain. Ye sensor nodes wireless network ke through ek central server ya cloud system ko data bhejte hain.

- **Types of WSN**:
    - **Homogeneous WSN**: Sare sensor nodes identical hote hain aur same tareeke se kaam karte hain.
    - **Heterogeneous WSN**: Sensor nodes ka functionality alag-alag hota hai.
    - **Mobile WSN**: Sensor nodes khud move kar sakte hain aur location change kar sakte hain.
- **Features**:

- **Energy Efficiency**: WSNs ko low power pe chalane ke liye design kiya jata hai.
- **Scalability**: Network ko easily scale up kiya ja sakta hai by adding more nodes.
- **Autonomous Operation**: Nodes khud se operate karte hain bina human interference ke.

- **Advantages**:
    - **Remote Monitoring**: Hard-to-reach locations se data collect kar sakte hain.
    - **Low Cost**: Sensor nodes affordable hote hain aur easily deploy kiye ja sakte hain.
    - **Real-time Data**: Data real-time collect hota hai aur analysis ke liye bheja jata hai.

- **Disadvantages**:
    - **Limited Battery Life**: Sensor nodes battery pe kaam karte hain, aur unki lifespan limited hoti hai.
    - **Network Reliability**: Agar sensor node fail ho jata hai to network unstable ho sakta hai.

- **Data Overload**: Large-scale networks mein collected data ko process karna mushkil ho sakta hai.

IoT Design Methodology: Specification - Requirement, Process, Model, Service, Functional & Operational View

- The **IoT Design Methodology** is a structured approach to designing and developing IoT systems. This methodology ensures that the IoT system meets the desired specifications, performs efficiently, and provides necessary services. It involves a sequence of steps that include identifying requirements, defining processes, creating models, and focusing on both functional and operational views.

- Let's break it down in detail:

1. Specification - Requirement

- **Definition**:

    The **Specification** phase of the IoT design methodology focuses on understanding and documenting what is needed from the system. This step includes identifying user needs, technological requirements, and system functionalities.

- **Key components** of this phase include:

- **User Requirements**: Understanding what the user needs from the IoT system (e.g., smart homes, industrial monitoring, etc.).

- **System Requirements**: Determining the hardware, software, and network requirements to meet user needs.

- **Functional Requirements**: What functionalities the IoT system should perform (e.g., sensor data collection, real-time analysis).

- **Non-functional Requirements**: These include scalability, reliability, security, and efficiency.

- **Example**:

  If you are designing an IoT system for a smart home, the specification could include requirements like monitoring temperature, controlling lights, and integrating with voice assistants.

2. Process

- **Definition**:

  The **Process** phase defines the sequence of steps and methodologies used to design, implement, and deploy the IoT system. It ensures that all requirements are met and the system functions as expected.

- **Steps in the process**:

    - **Research and Feasibility Study**: Conduct a study to understand if the IoT solution is feasible.

    - **Prototyping**: Develop a prototype to test the initial concept.

    - **System Development**: Once the prototype is successful, move on to the actual development of the system.

    - **Testing**: The system is rigorously tested to ensure it meets all the defined specifications and works as intended.

    - **Deployment and Monitoring**: After testing, the IoT system is deployed, and its performance is continuously monitored for improvements.

- **Example**:

    For a smart thermostat, the process would start with understanding the user's heating and cooling needs, designing the system, building a prototype, testing with various temperatures, and then deploying it to homes.

3. Model

- **Definition**:

    The **Model** phase refers to creating a conceptual or functional model of the IoT system. This model represents how the devices, sensors, and networks interact and how data flows between them.

- **Key aspects**:

    - **Device Models**: The model of devices involved in the IoT system (e.g., sensors, actuators).

    - **Communication Models**: Defining how devices communicate with each other and the central system (e.g., using protocols like MQTT, HTTP, or CoAP).

    - **Data Flow Model**: Defines how data will flow from sensors to data storage or analytics systems.

    - **Interaction Models**: Defines how users will interact with the system (e.g., mobile apps or voice assistants).

- **Example**:

    In a smart agriculture system, the model would describe how soil moisture sensors collect data and send it to a cloud server for analysis.

4. Service

- **Definition**:

    The **Service** phase involves defining the services that will be provided by the IoT system. These services include data collection, processing, and delivery to users. The service must be user-friendly and scalable.

- **Service Components**:

    - **Data Collection**: How the system collects data from sensors.

    - **Data Processing**: The system's ability to process and analyze collected data.

    - **Data Delivery**: How the processed data is delivered to users or other systems (e.g., through a mobile app or web dashboard).

- **User Interface**: How users interact with the IoT system (e.g., an app for controlling lights).

- **Example**:

In a smart city traffic management system, the service might include real-time traffic monitoring, control of traffic lights, and alerts for traffic congestion via an app.

5. Functional & Operational View

- **Definition**:
The **Functional View** and **Operational View** describe the system's capabilities and its performance in real-world scenarios.

- **Functional View**:
    - Focuses on what the IoT system can do (i.e., its functionalities).
    - It looks at the tasks that need to be performed to fulfill user needs.
    - Example: A system that controls street lights based on motion or brightness levels.

- **Operational View**:

- o Focuses on how the system performs in practice, considering reliability, scalability, and operational efficiency.

- o It includes how well the system handles real-world conditions, such as traffic congestion or extreme weather.

- o Example: In a smart home, how efficiently the system responds to user commands, even when multiple devices are in use.

Hindi Explanation (Hinglish)

IoT Design Methodology: Specification - Requirement, Process, Model, Service, Functional & Operational View

- **Definition**:
  IoT design methodology ek structured tareeka hai, jo IoT system ko design aur develop karne ke liye use kiya jata hai. Is methodology ka main goal hota hai ki IoT system jo bhi requirements hain, unhe puri kare, efficiently work kare, aur zaruri services provide kare.

- Chaliye, ise thoda detail mein samajhte hain:

1. Specification - Requirement

- **Definition**:
  Specification phase mein hum system ki zarurat ko samajhte hain aur document karte hain. Is step mein user ki needs, technology ki requirements, aur system ki functionalities ko define kiya jata hai.

- **Key components**:

  - **User Requirements**: Users ko kis cheez ki zarurat hai (jaise smart homes, industrial monitoring, etc.)?

  - **System Requirements**: Humare system ke liye kaunse hardware, software, aur network ki zarurat hogi.

  - **Functional Requirements**: System ko kis tarah ki functionalities perform karni chahiye (jaise sensor data collection, real-time analysis).

  - **Non-functional Requirements**: Scalability, reliability, security, aur efficiency jaisi cheezein.

- **Example**:
  Agar aap smart home ka IoT system design kar rahe hain, to

specification mein temperature monitoring, light control, aur voice assistants ke integration ka requirement ho sakta hai.

2. Process

- **Definition**:

  Process phase mein hum steps define karte hain jo IoT system ko design, develop, aur deploy karte waqt follow karne padte hain. Yeh ensure karta hai ki saari requirements meet ho rahi hain aur system efficiently work kar raha hai.

- **Steps in the process**:

  - **Research and Feasibility Study**: Pehle research ki jaati hai, taaki samajh sakein ki IoT solution feasible hai ya nahi.

  - **Prototyping**: Ek initial prototype design kiya jata hai taaki concept ko test kiya ja sake.

  - **System Development**: Jab prototype successful hota hai, tab actual development hota hai.

  - **Testing**: System ko test kiya jata hai taaki ye ensure ho sake ki system jo kaam kar raha hai, wo specifications ke according hai.

- o **Deployment and Monitoring**: Testing ke baad system ko deploy kiya jata hai aur performance continuously monitor ki jati hai.

- **Example**:

  Smart thermostat ke design process mein user ki heating aur cooling needs samajhna, design banana, prototype build karna, aur testing ke baad deployment shamil hoga.

3. Model

- **Definition**:

  Model phase mein hum IoT system ka conceptual ya functional model create karte hain. Ye model batata hai ki devices, sensors, aur networks kaise interact karte hain aur data ka flow kis tarah se hoga.

- **Key aspects**:

  - o **Device Models**: IoT system mein jo devices involve hain, unka model.

  - o **Communication Models**: Ye define karta hai ki devices ke beech aur central system ke beech communication kaise hoga.

- **Data Flow Model**: Data ka flow sensor se cloud ya storage tak kaise hoga, yeh define kiya jata hai.

- **Interaction Models**: Ye batata hai ki users kaise system se interact karenge (app ya voice assistants ke through).

- **Example**:
  Smart agriculture system mein model dikhayega ki kaise soil moisture sensors data collect karte hain aur cloud server par analysis ke liye bhejte hain.

4. Service

- **Definition**:
  Service phase mein wo services define ki jati hain jo IoT system ke through provide ki jayengi. Yeh services data collection, processing, aur users tak delivery se related hoti hain.

- **Service Components**:

  - **Data Collection**: Kaise system data ko sensors se collect karega.

  - **Data Processing**: Kaise data ko process aur analyze kiya jayega.

- **Data Delivery**: Processed data ko users ya dusre systems tak kaise deliver kiya jayega.
- **User Interface**: Users kaise system se interact karenge (app ke through, web dashboard).

- **Example**:
Smart city traffic management system mein service include kar sakti hai real-time traffic monitoring, traffic lights ka control, aur traffic congestion ke alerts mobile app ke through.

5. Functional & Operational View

- **Definition**:
Functional aur Operational view system ki capabilities aur real-world performance ko define karte hain.

- **Functional View**:
    - Yeh batata hai ki IoT system kya kar sakta hai (functions).
    - Yeh tasks ko define karta hai jo system ko perform karne hote hain.
    - Example: Ek system jo motion aur brightness ke basis pe street lights control karta hai.

- **Operational View**:

- Yeh batata hai ki system real-world mein kaise perform karega. Yeh reliability, scalability, aur efficiency ko focus karta hai.
- Example: Smart home mein system kaise respond karega jab multiple devices ek saath use ho rahe ho.

IoT Privacy and Security Solutions

Definition:

IoT privacy and security solutions aim to protect the data generated by IoT devices and ensure that the communication and processes are secure. Since IoT devices often handle sensitive information, ensuring their security and privacy is a critical part of their design.

- **Privacy Solutions**:
    - Protecting sensitive user information from unauthorized access.
    - Examples: Encryption, secure authentication, and access control.

- **Security Solutions**:
    - Ensuring that IoT devices, networks, and data transmissions are protected against hacking, cyber-attacks, and other threats.
    - Examples: Firewalls, intrusion detection systems, and secure communication protocols like HTTPS, VPNs.

- **Types of Security Measures**:

- **Data Encryption**: Ensures that data transmitted by IoT devices is unreadable to unauthorized users.

- **Authentication and Authorization**: Ensures that only authorized users can access the system.

- **Firewalls**: Protects the IoT network from unauthorized access.

- **Intrusion Detection Systems (IDS)**: Detects any unauthorized access or malicious activities within the system.

- **Challenges**:

  - **Scalability**: Ensuring privacy and security as the number of IoT devices grows.

  - **Resource Constraints**: Many IoT devices are low-power, which can limit the implementation of advanced security solutions.

  - **Interoperability**: Ensuring security across devices and platforms that may not always follow the same standards.

Explaintation in Hinglish

IoT Privacy and Security Solutions

Definition:

IoT privacy aur security solutions ka main goal ye hota hai ki IoT devices se generate hone wale data ko protect kiya ja sake aur communication aur processes ko secure banaya ja sake. IoT devices sensitive data handle karte hain, isliye unki security aur privacy ka dhyaan rakhna bahut zaroori hota hai.

- **Privacy Solutions**:

    o Sensitive user information ko unauthorized access se protect karna.

    o Examples: Data encryption, secure authentication, aur access control.

- **Security Solutions**:

    o Ye ensure karna ki IoT devices, networks, aur data transmissions hacking aur cyber attacks se secure ho.

    o Examples: Firewalls, intrusion detection systems, aur secure communication protocols jaise HTTPS, VPNs.

- **Types of Security Measures**:

    - **Data Encryption**: Ye ensure karta hai ki jo data IoT devices se transmit hota hai, wo unauthorized users ke liye unreadable ho.

    - **Authentication and Authorization**: Ye ensure karta hai ki sirf authorized users hi system ko access kar sakein.

    - **Firewalls**: Ye IoT network ko unauthorized access se protect karte hain.

    - **Intrusion Detection Systems (IDS)**: Ye system ke andar unauthorized access ya malicious activities ko detect karte hain.

- **Challenges**:

    - **Scalability**: Jaise-jaise IoT devices ki sankhya badhti hai, waise-waise privacy aur security ko maintain karna mushkil ho sakta hai.

    - **Resource Constraints**: Kai IoT devices low-power pe kaam karte hain, isliye advanced security solutions ko implement karna challenging ho sakta hai.

- **Interoperability**: Alag-alag devices aur platforms ke beech security standards ka match karna mushkil ho sakta hai.

Raspberry Pi & Arduino Devices for IoT

- **Raspberry Pi** and **Arduino** are two widely used devices in the Internet of Things (IoT) projects. These devices play an important role in developing IoT applications by acting as central controllers or interface units for sensors, actuators, and communication modules.

Raspberry Pi:

- **Definition**: Raspberry Pi is a small, affordable, single-board computer that is widely used for IoT applications.

- **Key Features**:
    - **Low Cost**: It is an inexpensive device, making it accessible for all users.

- **GPIO Pins**: Raspberry Pi has General Purpose Input/Output (GPIO) pins that allow it to interact with external devices like sensors, motors, and other electronic components.

- **Powerful Processing**: Raspberry Pi provides more processing power compared to Arduino and supports a variety of operating systems (including Linux-based).

- **Connectivity**: It supports Wi-Fi, Ethernet, and Bluetooth connectivity, which is crucial for IoT applications.

- **Example Uses**:

- Smart Home Automation: Control lights, fans, and security systems.

- Weather Station: Collect data from environmental sensors and display it on a dashboard.

Arduino:

- **Definition**: Arduino is an open-source electronics platform based on simple software and hardware. It is a microcontroller that can be programmed to interact with various sensors and devices.

- **Key Features**:

    - **Simplicity**: Arduino is designed for beginners, with an easy-to-use programming environment.

    - **GPIO Pins**: Like Raspberry Pi, Arduino also has GPIO pins that can be used to connect with sensors and actuators.

    - **Real-time Operations**: Arduino is excellent for real-time control and interactions in IoT applications.

    - **Low Power Consumption**: Arduino is more power-efficient than Raspberry Pi, making it ideal for battery-powered applications.

- **Example Uses**:

- Home Automation: Control lights and temperature using sensors.

- Monitoring Systems: Collect sensor data and send it to cloud platforms for analysis.

Advantages and Disadvantages:

- **Raspberry Pi:**

- **Advantages**:

- More powerful and flexible.
- Supports multiple programming languages.
- Can run full-fledged operating systems, making it more suitable for complex IoT applications.

- **Disadvantages**:
    - Higher power consumption.
    - Needs more advanced setup (e.g., keyboard, mouse, and monitor for setup).

Arduino:

- **Advantages**:
    - Simple to use and highly customizable.
    - Low power consumption, ideal for battery-powered applications.
    - Extensive community support.

- **Disadvantages**:
    - Limited processing power and memory.

- Does not support complex tasks like running full operating systems.

Hindi Explanation (Hinglish)

Raspberry Pi & Arduino Devices in IoT

- **1. Raspberry Pi:**

- **Definition**: Raspberry Pi ek chhota, affordable computer hai jo IoT applications mein use hota hai. Yeh ek single-board computer hai jise sensors, actuators, aur communication modules ke saath connect kiya ja sakta hai.

- **Features**:

    - **Low Cost**: Yeh kaafi sasta hota hai aur sabhi ko accessible hai.

    - **GPIO Pins**: Raspberry Pi mein GPIO pins hote hain jinke through external devices ko control kiya ja sakta hai, jaise sensors, motors, etc.

    - **Powerful Processing**: Raspberry Pi mein zyada processing power hoti hai aur yeh Linux-based operating systems ko support karta hai.

- **Connectivity**: Ismein Wi-Fi, Ethernet, aur Bluetooth connectivity hoti hai, jo IoT applications ke liye important hai.

- **Example Uses**:

- **Smart Home Automation**: Lights, fans, aur security systems ko control karna.

- **Weather Station**: Environmental sensors se data collect karna aur dashboard par display karna.

- **2. Arduino:**

- **Definition**: Arduino ek open-source electronics platform hai jo simple software aur hardware pe based hota hai. Yeh ek microcontroller hai jo sensors aur devices ke saath interact karne ke liye program kiya ja sakta hai.

- **Features**:

    - **Simplicity**: Arduino beginners ke liye design kiya gaya hai aur iska programming environment kaafi easy hai.

    - **GPIO Pins**: Arduino mein bhi GPIO pins hote hain jo sensors aur actuators ke saath connect karne ke liye use kiye ja sakte hain.

- o **Real-time Operations**: Arduino IoT applications mein real-time control aur interaction ke liye best hai.

- o **Low Power Consumption**: Raspberry Pi ke comparison mein Arduino ka power consumption kaafi kam hota hai, isliye yeh battery-powered applications ke liye ideal hai.

- **Example Uses**:

- **Home Automation**: Lights aur temperature ko sensors ke through control karna.

- **Monitoring Systems**: Sensor data collect karna aur cloud platforms par send karna.

Advantages and Disadvantages:

- **Raspberry Pi:**

- **Advantages**:

  - o Zyada powerful aur flexible hota hai.
  - o Multiple programming languages support karta hai.
  - o Full operating systems ko run kar sakta hai, jo complex IoT applications ke liye zaruri hai.

- **Disadvantages**:
    - Zyada power consume karta hai.
    - Setup thoda complex hota hai, kyunki isko setup karte waqt keyboard, mouse aur monitor ki zarurat padti hai.

- **Arduino:**

- **Advantages**:
    - Simple aur highly customizable hota hai.
    - Low power consumption, isliye battery-powered applications ke liye perfect hai.
    - Extensive community support available hoti hai.

- **Disadvantages**:
    - Limited processing power aur memory hoti hai.
    - Full operating systems run nahi kar sakta, isliye complex tasks ke liye suitable nahi hota.

IoT Case Study: Smart City Streetlights Control & Monitoring

- A **Smart City Streetlight Control & Monitoring** system is an IoT application that automates and optimizes streetlight management. By using IoT devices and sensors, it ensures that streetlights are only on when needed, thus saving energy and reducing operational costs.

- **Components**:

- **Sensors**: Light sensors detect whether there is sufficient natural light. Motion sensors detect movement in the streets, ensuring lights are on when people or vehicles pass by.

- **Communication Protocols**: These sensors send data to a central system using wireless communication protocols like Wi-Fi, Zigbee, or LoRaWAN.

- **Control Systems**: A central system that analyzes the data and controls the streetlight operations remotely. It can adjust the brightness based on time, weather conditions, and street activity.

- **Benefits**:

- **Energy Savings**: Streetlights operate only when necessary, reducing energy consumption.

- **Maintenance Alerts**: If a light is malfunctioning, the system sends an alert to the maintenance team.

- **Cost-Efficiency**: Reduces manual monitoring and maintenance costs.

Hindi Explanation (Hinglish)

IoT Case Study: Smart City Streetlights Control & Monitoring

- **Smart City Streetlight Control & Monitoring** system ek IoT application hai jo streetlight management ko automate aur optimize karta hai. IoT devices aur sensors ka use karke yeh ensure karta hai ki streetlights tabhi on ho jab zarurat ho, jisse energy bachti hai aur operational costs reduce hoti hain.

- **Components**:

- **Sensors**: Light sensors natural light ko detect karte hain aur motion sensors streets mein movement detect karte hain, jisse lights unke paas se guzarne par on ho jati hain.

- **Communication Protocols**: Yeh sensors data ko ek central system tak bhejte hain wireless communication protocols jaise Wi-Fi, Zigbee, ya LoRaWAN ke through.

- **Control Systems**: Central system data ko analyze karta hai aur streetlight operations ko remotely control karta hai. Yeh time, weather conditions, aur street activity ke hisaab se brightness adjust kar sakta hai.

- **Benefits**:

- **Energy Savings**: Streetlights sirf tabhi on hoti hain jab zarurat ho, jisse energy consume kam hoti hai.

- **Maintenance Alerts**: Agar koi light malfunction kar rahi ho, to system automatically maintenance team ko alert bhejta hai.

- **Cost-Efficiency**: Manual monitoring aur maintenance costs reduce ho jati hain.

www.ingramcontent.com/pod-product-compliance
Lightning Source LLC
Chambersburg PA
CBHW082251220526
45469CB00009B/2955